Pratima Mitchell was born in India and first began a career
as a journalist and feature writer in New Delhi. She now writes
and teaches in Oxford. Her previous books for children include
*The Ramayana, Rich or Poor?, Still Waters, Grandfather Singh Stories,
Gandhi, Dance of Shiva, Indian Mutiny, The Guru's Family*
and the Minnie stories.

Caroline Binch has illustrated children's books for Rosa Guy,
Oralee Wachter and Grace Nichols as well as writing and illustrating
a number of her own titles. Her illustrations for Rita Phillips Mitchell's
Hue Boy and *Down by the River* were shortlisted for the Kate Greenaway Medal
in 1993 and 1996, with *Hue Boy* going on to win the Smarties Prize.
Caroline is perhaps best known for illustrating Mary Hoffman's bestselling
picture books *Amazing Grace*, which was shortlisted for the Kate Greenaway
Medal, and *Grace & Family,* and the storybook *Starring Grace*, which are all
published by Frances Lincoln. Her other Frances Lincoln titles are *Since Dad Left*,
winner of the United Kingdom Book Award in 1998, and *Silver Shoes*,
shortlisted for the Kate Greenaway Medal in 2002.

For Priya, my violinist daughter – P.M.

For Senka and Bisera – C.B.

Petar's Song copyright © Frances Lincoln Limited 2003
Text copyright © Pratima Mitchell 2003
Illustrations copyright © Caroline Binch 2003
The right of Pratima Mitchell to be identified as the author of this work has been asserted
by her in accordance with the Copyright, Designs and Patents Act, 1988 (United Kingdom).

First published in Great Britain and the USA in 2003 by
Frances Lincoln Children's Books, 4 Torriano Mews,
Torriano Avenue, London NW5 2RZ
www.franceslincoln.com

Distributed in the USA by Publishers Group West

First paperback edition 2003

British Library Cataloguing in Publication Data available on request

ISBN 978-1-84507-352-7

Illustrated with watercolours

Set in Bembo

Printed in Singapore

5 7 9 8 6 4

Petar's Song

Pratima Mitchell
Illustrated by Caroline Binch

F

FRANCES LINCOLN
CHILDREN'S BOOKS

When Petar played his violin, everyone listened. Whenever there was a celebration – Christmas, Easter, sowing and harvest, weddings and birthdays – Petar and the children went through the village singing and dancing. Petar always led the procession, drawing out melodies and setting everyone's feet tapping to his jigs and polkas.

At Christmas time, Petar's father conducted the village choir.
His deep voice would ring out in the frosty night air: "Silent night!
Holy night!" When the children sang with him, their mouths
opened wide and caught the falling snowflakes which melted on
their tongues. Pine, candlewax and the rich
aroma of cinnamon cake scented the air.
It was a happy place.

One autumn evening, Petar was herding the cows home
from the high pasture and trying out a new tune on his fiddle.
Suddenly a loud explosion shattered the air. The cows and Petar
nearly jumped out of their skins.

Petar ran back up the hillside to see what was happening.
His heart turned a somersault as the rat-tat-tat of gunfire
bounced off neighbouring mountainsides.

He tried to round up the cows by playing their favourite
going-home tune, but it was drowned by the noise of church
bells crashing and jangling their terrible news – war had begun.

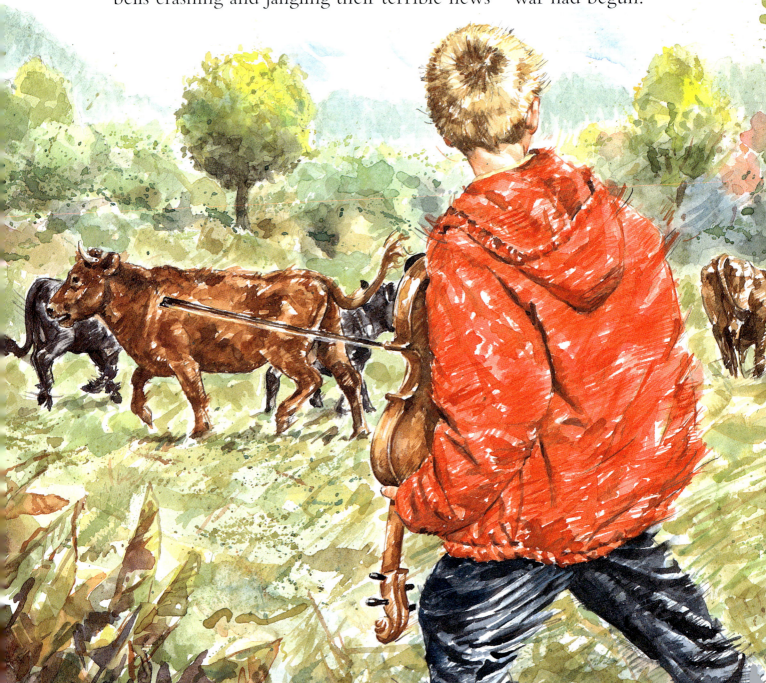

Long after Petar had gone to bed, he heard the murmur
of his parents' voices. They talked far into the night.

At dawn, Petar's father packed food and water.
He and Mother rolled up blankets and strapped them
on four rucksacks.

"Get ready, all of you. Go west." Father pointed to the other side of the mountains. "You'll be safe there. I'll follow as soon as I can." Petar, Gregor and Anna clung to him and wouldn't let go.

"Who will take care of you now?"
Petar whispered to his favourite cow.

As they set off up the hill, Father came running after them.

"Petar, you've forgotten your violin!" He gave him the case.

"Look after your mother, Gregor and Anna."

Then he went back to join the other men.

Night fell swiftly. They tried to stay invisible by keeping to the shadows. Spurts of red and orange flames in the valleys signalled houses on fire. Shells exploded in the distance. The wind howled and the forest crackled with menacing noises. They pressed on without stopping.

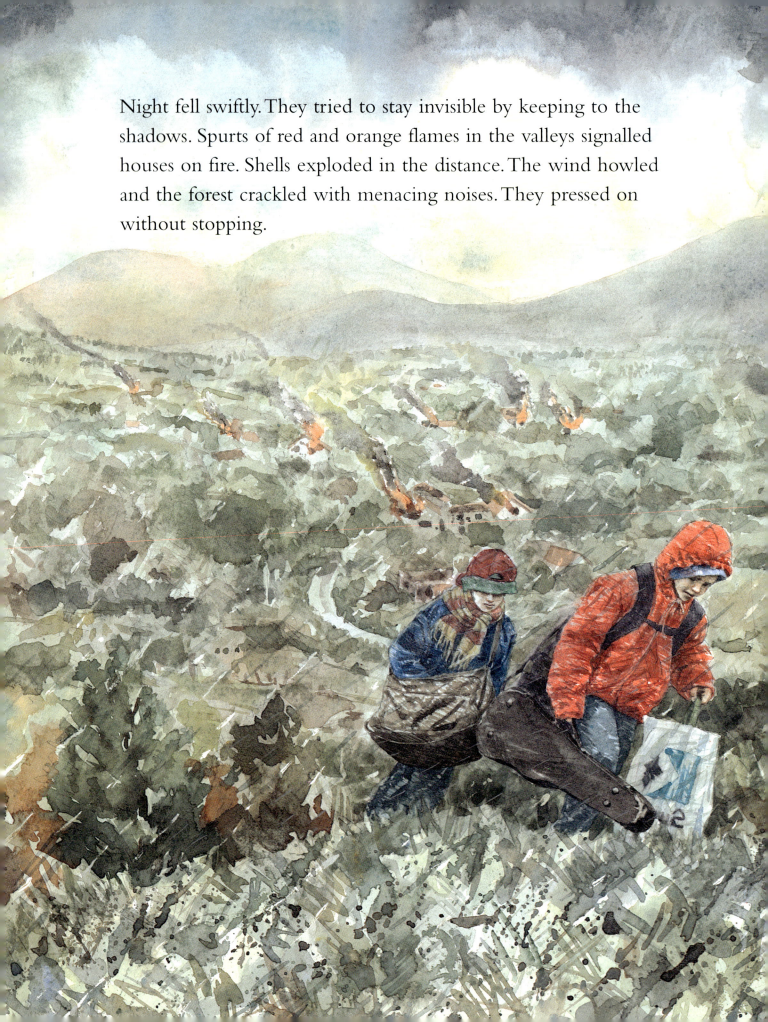

Three days later they crossed the border and reached a safe town. Their stomachs were empty and their feet were blistered and sore. The streets were full of other refugees looking for food and shelter. Children were begging for bread, and Petar saw a man snatch an apple from a market stall.

"Petar, play your violin," said Anna. "People will give you money, and we can buy food." But Petar couldn't play. His fingers felt stiff, like clothes pegs. There were no songs in his heart now.

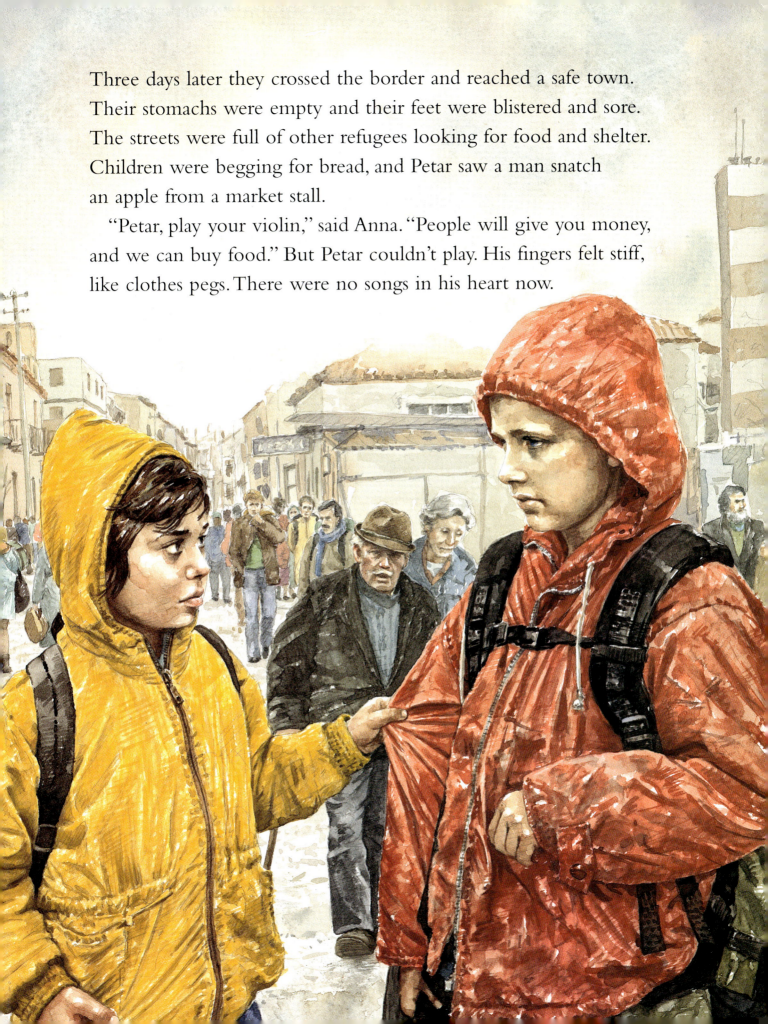

Mother made a place to sleep in a doorway.
All night the snow fell. It was very cold.
Petar remembered how Father used to sing.

He remembered his friends saying, "Petar, play your violin!"
He shut his eyes and imagined they were all sitting in front
of the fire, roasting nuts. At last he fell asleep.

The next day, a kind man let them move into
his garden shed. He fetched beds, a table and a chair,
and made it warm and cosy. He even gave Mother
a job in the café. "I hope you'll be happy here," he
said. But how could they be happy without Father?

It was nearly Christmas. Anna and
Gregor borrowed scissors and paper
and glue to make cards to send to
Father. But Petar didn't feel like making
anything. What was there to celebrate?

The streets were deserted. Everyone was indoors cooking, wrapping presents and getting ready for Christmas Eve.

Petar marched – left, right, left, right. Where was Father now? Was he in danger? Was he marching down an icy road? Was he singing "Silent Night"?

Petar started to hum the tune to himself.

All of a sudden, a new melody came to Petar, a dancing rhythm, a tune to welcome the spring. He closed his eyes, searching for words that would fit. When he opened them, snowflakes were whirling down like tiny dancers. He tried out the tune in his head. Then he sang it out loud. Snowflakes floated into his open mouth and melted on his tongue.

He ran back to the garden shed. Where was it? Where had he put it?

There it was, in a basket of newly-laundered clothes. He opened the case and tenderly lifted out his violin. Then he picked up the bow and began to tune the strings.

Moments later, the sweetest of sounds reached the café. His little sister Anna cried, "Listen – Petar's playing again!"

Mother dried her hands. One by one, the customers left their food and came outside. Then they began to clap and snap their fingers.

Petar played all his favourite tunes,
one by one. Everyone linked arms and danced
the old jigs and polkas and waltzes. They laughed and hugged
each other. "Happy Christmas!" they cried.

Petar smiled. Suddenly he thought, "I can give Father something for Christmas! I'll give him my new song. I know we'll be together again, some day."

He hugged Mother, Gregor and Anna.

"Let's make a wish," he said. And just then, the words of his song came to him:

When swallows fly across the sun,
When Earth has woken up from sleep,
We'll sow the seed and beg the wind
To carry a song of peace.

MORE TITLES FROM
FRANCES LINCOLN CHILDREN'S BOOKS

Silver Shoes
Caroline Binch

Molly loves to dance, and she desperately wants some silver shoes
to wear to her first dance class. But her mum says she has to wait
and see if she likes the classes first. Nearly all the other girls are
wearing silver shoes, even Molly's best friend!

ISBN 978-1-84507-471-5

Christy's Dream
Caroline Binch

Christy has wanted a pony for as long as he can remember.
Lots of other boys on the estate have their own horses, so now
Christy's saved up enough money no-one can stop him making
his dream come true. But what will his ma say when he
brings his new horse home?

ISBN 978-1-84507-472-2

Since Dad Left
Caroline Binch

Sid feels cross. He doesn't understand why his mum and dad –
Sandra and Mick – don't live together any more. And when Sandra
tells Sid she's arranged for him to spend the day with Mick,
he doesn't want to go. But Mick's offbeat way of life turns out
to be very different from most people's and Sid can't help
being drawn towards it…

ISBN 978-0-7112-1355-5

Frances Lincoln titles are available from all good bookshops.
You can also buy books and find out more about your favourite titles,
authors and illustrators on our website: www.franceslincoln.com